BODY PARTS

Learning Props, L.L.C.

head

hair

cheek

chin

neck

face

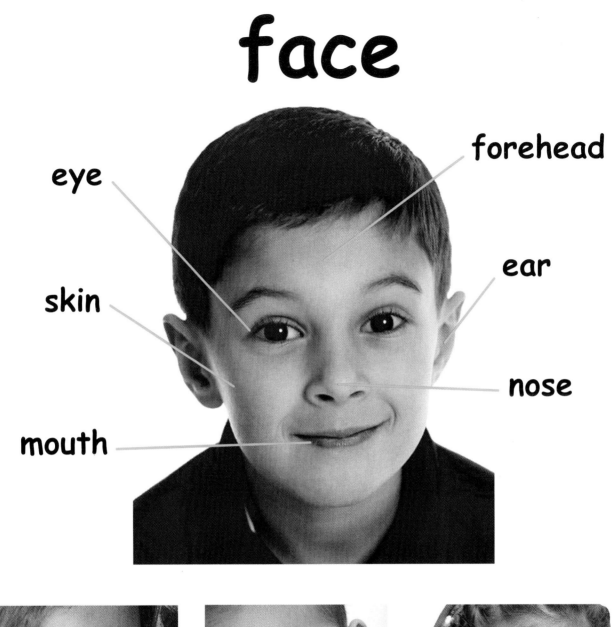

forehead

eye

ear

skin

nose

mouth

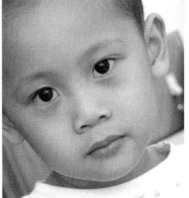

eye

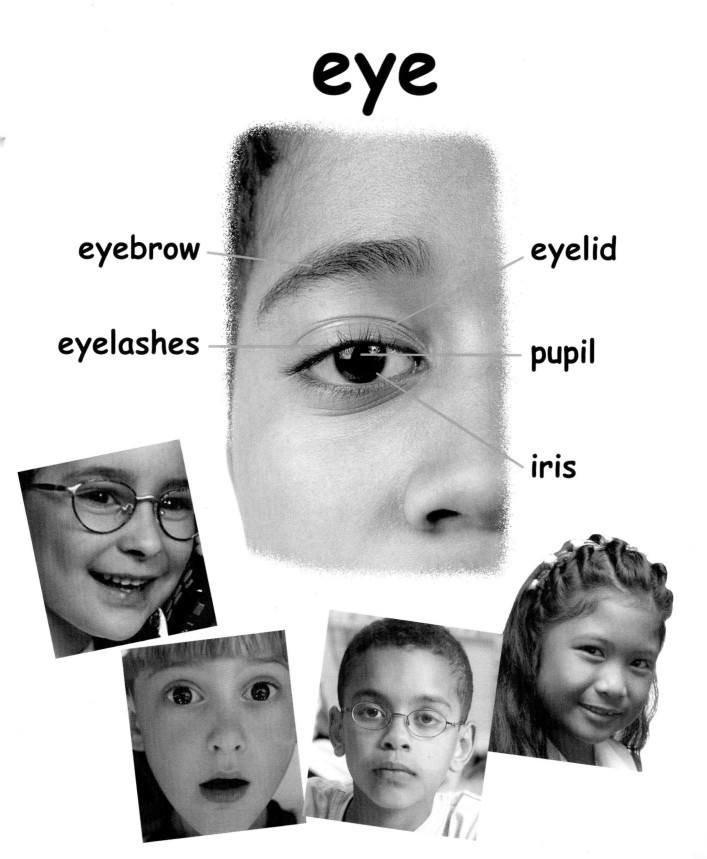

eyebrow

eyelid

eyelashes

pupil

iris

ear

earlobe

mouth

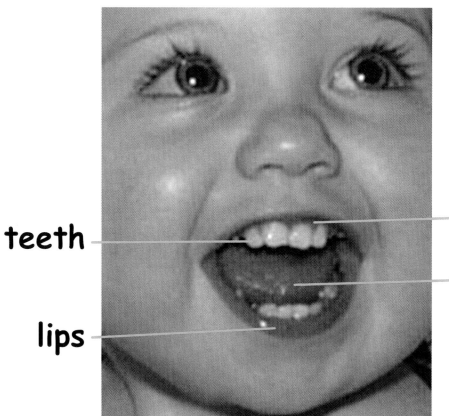

teeth

gums

tongue

lips

hair

red hair

black hair

blonde hair

brown hair

straight hair

curly hair

nose

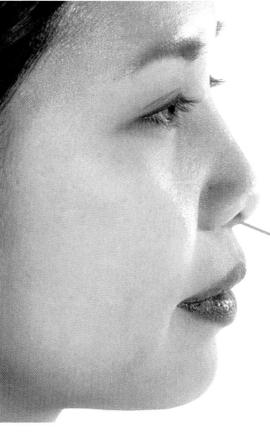

nostril

arm

hand

elbow

shoulder

wrist

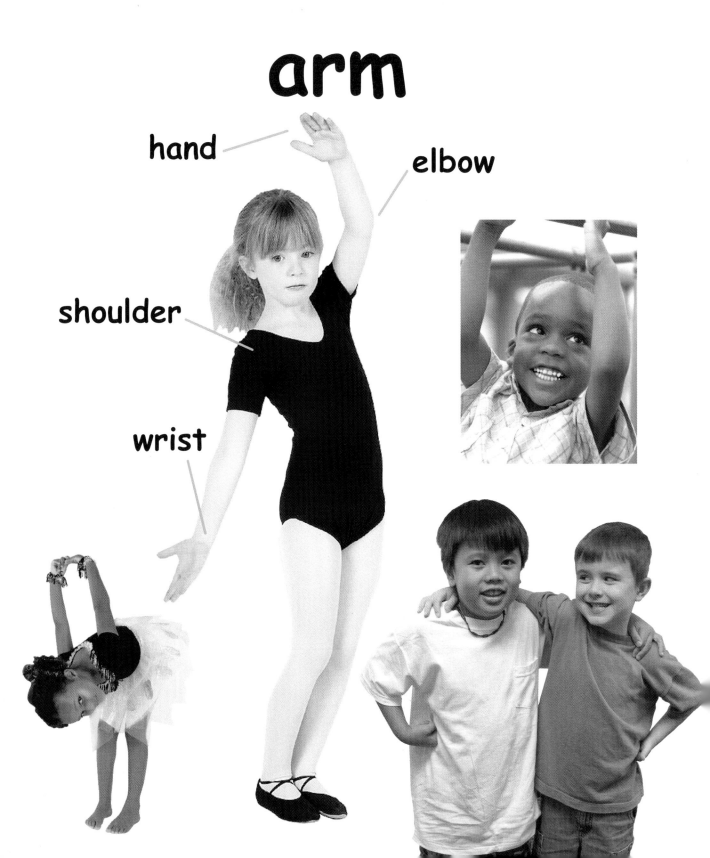

hand

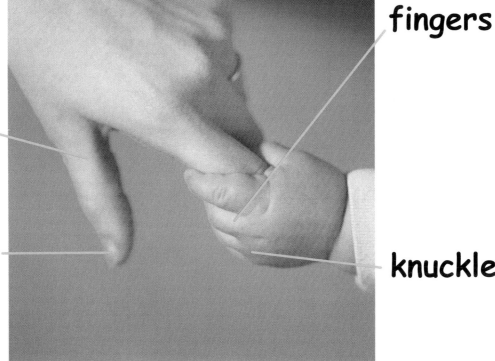

fingers

thumb

fingernail

knuckle

palm

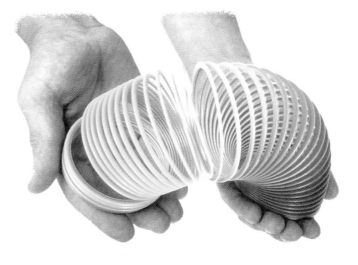

leg

foot

ankle

shin

calf

thigh

knee

hip

foot

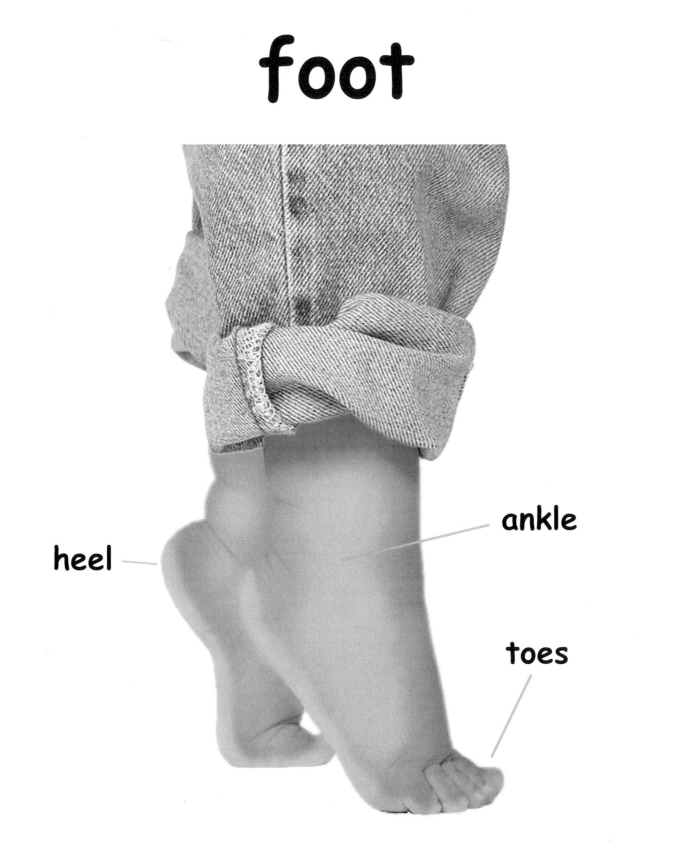

ankle

heel

toes

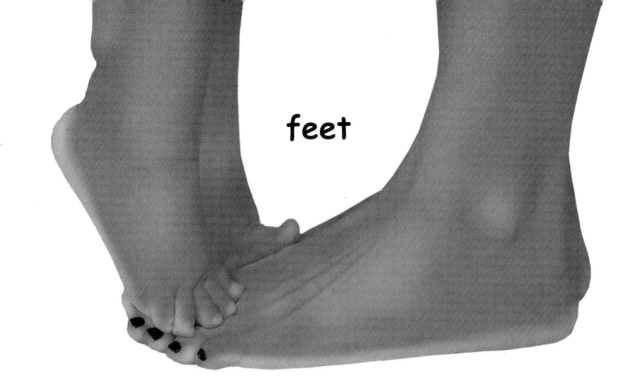

feet

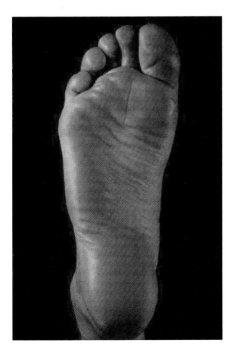

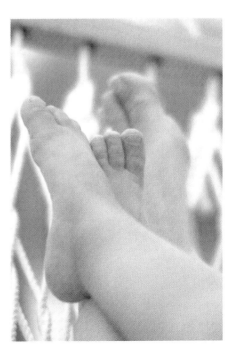

elbow

shoulder

chest

stomach

waist

hip

chest

back

bottom

Which body parts can you name on these animals?

find the body parts